POEMS IN THE TIME OF COVID

BY THERESA JONES — AND OTHER TIMES

Brigand
London

Brigand Press
All contact: info@brigand.london
Cover Michelle Ruffieux, Blush Design.

British Library Cataloguing-in-Publication Data
A catalogue record for this book is
available from the British Library
Printed and Bound in Great Britain by
Datum Creative Media Limited.

ISBN: 978-1-912978-36-6

I first got to know Theresa when she was teaching English and Religious Education in the Chelmsley Wood area of Solihull. She taught in Smith's Wood and Whitesmore Secondary Schools, both challenging, exacting learning environments. She was an excellent classroom teacher, kindly but firm with her pupils and always thoroughly on top of her material. Even then, and this was many years ago, Theresa wrote poetry. Back then she had a quite elaborate style, favouring rhyme schemes and often regular rhythms.

About twenty years ago a poetry writing group came together in Solihull. We called our group Writers' Cramp and Theresa became one of its first members. Since then she has been an assiduous and enthusiastic attendee of almost every one of our meetings and we try to meet roughly once every six weeks.

Theresa's poetic style has become very distinctive over the years. She writes with unusual clarity, giving every word she uses its full weight and wasting none. There is never any unnecessary language in her poems. She relies on the power of very carefully chosen nouns and verbs, rarely using adjectives or adverbs. The consequence is poetry that has impressive lucidity and authority. It stands on the page clean and unvarnished.

Her themes are usually religious and there is always a strongly spiritual element to her poetry. Sometimes she takes a Biblical story for the spine of her poem; sometimes it is the references she makes to Biblical characters or the use to which she puts the work of philosophers who have influenced her thinking that give her work distinctive flavour.

Always Theresa's poetry carries conviction and impact. Often particular lines remain long in the memory. Often the full force of a poem will reside in its powerful last lines.

It is as though poetry for Theresa is a natural expression of her preoccupations and her emotions. The words feel as though they are transcribed directly from her unconscious mind on to the page. We fortunate readers are the recipients of poem after poem written in the heat of creation, full of stimulating thought and authentic emotion, expressed in translucent language.

David Curtis
Inspector LEA

Acknowledgements

Firstly, my grateful thanks must go to my poet friends, members of Writer's Cramp: David Curtis, Heather Harrison, Brian Chase, Glena Baptiste, Dallin Chapman and Pamela Vaughan, who by their encouragement and constructive criticism have helped me to maintain some discipline in 'turning out' a poem to present, on a given theme, at our regular poetry meetings.

This is not to deny that there have been lean times when no amount of effort can entice the Poetic Muse to bring inspiration. However, for the most part, rhythms and words present themselves in response to the theme without too much difficulty, laying aside the fact that it often happens in the middle of the night!

My thanks must also go to Freda Sumner, who offers an unending stream of appreciation and encouragement. To my son David, for the occasional word of inspiration. Michelle Ruffieux has been immensely helpful and patient in preparing the poems for publication and offering advice on artwork. My thanks also to Neil Survilla and Scott Pearce for help and guidance with publishing. Always ready with help and support has been my husband, Dave. I offer this work for him and for all who have learned to value the poetic voice.

Theresa Jones

Contents

Contents

The Fall 2020

We were the lotus eaters
drunk at times with apathy
survival seemingly secure
our world close at hand
no dread contagion
or anxious fears assailed

heedless of this future
we ate our fill
polluted and contaminated
sank our teeth into the earth
created our own downfall

yet, like our antediluvian parents
we continue on, this side of Eden
beneath a cirrocumulus mackerel sky

Away Day

Drawn from the melee of our secret lives
One of us, a Covid victim, being absent
We join together for this solitary day
Our common knowing, our common love
Igniting the joy and delight of poetry

Here in this ancient Manor House
Chilling, yet warmly welcoming
Receptive of our laughter, our silences
Our uninvited sighs our application
We await an outcome

Perhaps today we will succeed
Call forth the muse who will perform
Bring inspiration, fire imagination
Convince us we can dare to claim that wondrous title:
'Poet'

New Dawn

In the walled garden facing away from the sun
Watching the rose New Dawn coming into bud
The Passion Flower cut back making ready
to overwhelm with blooms
The Peace rose: free as yet of black spot
The little birch tree: a self-setter bringing hope
Sad daffodils droop dark brown heads
Saying goodbye to their year of Covid
In which they cheered the heart
The rose called Compassion yet to bud

The Green Handbag

Another victim of lockdown
the green handbag
In a boutique shop window
hanging there for months
So appealing – 'from Paris', it said
Certainly stylish, a trendsetter
Watched, day by day on the walk
secretly desired, longed for even
but set aside quietly... quite forgotten
But you noticed, waited patiently
Secretly turned up on opening day, early
but not early enough: sold to another!
Two days later, somewhere in the country
The same was found and posted, labelled 'surprise'!
Like the old wife in 'The King and I', I have to say:
"You may not always do what I would have you do
But then you'll do something wonderful, wonderful...
Because you're won-der-ful!"

The Vestry Door

This was no Ignatian Examen
more an evening reflection
a search through the day for that moment
which spoke
Aha... it was the vestry door
Locked against me, shielding the holy place
at ease of lockdown
Me the unclean
in an open but not quite church
alien, austere, and silent
Plastic chains cross the nave aisle
bar my way to the altar
no welcoming face, no heavenly choir
at ease of lockdown
just sanitizers, sprays and signage:
Thou shalt not! Thou shalt not!
The vestry door then found a voice
and called after me:
"As the people so the priest!"

Coronavirus 2020

Someone said: we need to repent –
confess, wear sackcloth and ashes
turn back...
No!
We're children of the Enlightenment
no one is punishing us
there's no revenge

Scientists – the prophets of today –
tell us: death lurks
ambivalence is exploited
wash your hands – keep your distance
consider others – lock down
Defy the destructive enemy
await herd immunity

In an Age of Reason
there's no plot – no reprisal
no forgiveness
just a lonely corporate guilt
and the virus: a logical outcome
a natural consequence of greed
which on this occasion
burst the bag

Barbara

She was always glad of company
grateful, to be in her own home
fearful of Covid
the scourge of old age

Yet she, trusting in Abraham's 'Jehovah Jirah'
'The God who provides'
found in the kindness and duty of others:
food, shower, cleaning
A cheerful smile
Rocked each day to patience
by time: Keats' 'aged nurse'

While her failing eyes scanned the garden
for new life
they prevented reading and the jig-saw
The radio, and the phone
a lifeline

Boris's Red Jacket

Boris (not Johnson)
A dachshund with a history
who lives nearby:
Short legs, intelligent attentive face
smooth shiny coat, cautiously friendly

A loved pet who enjoyed life
'til one day his mistress died
Boris kept watch, nudging gently
For three days
All alone
striving to wake the dead
Try not to imagine the scene

A new owner took him on
Opened to him her home and garden
Gave him walks at 'lockdown'
Bought him a red jacket
To guard against the winter's cold
Advertised on Amazon as:
'Warm, lightweight, bright'

If Boris reflected
He might say:
There is a higher power
that protects, in spite of all

Things are Different

Tectonic plates of existence shift
boundaries dissolve and disappear
as energy is released
a rebalancing takes place
The earth and its people adjust
to ground shaking, destabilisation and aftershock
Expect the unexpected –
as we move on the cakewalk of life

One prophet said: 'fear is on every side'
and would we believe one who said:
'there are no children in the streets'
Contagion and danger await us on every corner
the contaminated indiscernible from the pure
Covid, the invisible terrorist, rivalling humanity
opposing an obscure and hidden God

St. Cecilia

The warmth of summertime Roma
In the Trastevere area
nurtured the martyr's palm
that grew in honour of Cecilia
As she piously bent her head

Music played amidst the waiting crowds
And the day had a celebratory feel
Bread and wine flowed
For those whose time had not yet come

'Who can find a virtuous woman?'
Questioned Solomon
We could nominate Cecilia
Giving up her marriage consummation
With the tolerant Valerian
In order to keep a vow

How does Christianity fare today?
Empty convents and monasteries betray
Our materialism: our non-commitment
Is the exchange a worthy one?
Why has faith died or ceased to attract?

Queen's College Chapel
Birmingham

The best is in the silence
where the prayers of years are felt
in the struggles that have been there
and the answers that are dealt

Take your seat and start your waiting
meet whatever comes your way
in your spirit search the corners
and be thankful for this day

Look about you at the image
of the ox and eagle there
see the pelican and angel
and the lion if you dare

Greet each new encounter
let it come and let it go
there's a purpose in this stillness
for your weal or for your woe

When you rise to take your journey
you will know that you have been
in a place where Ancient Wisdom
can be sensed and even seen

Caravaggio: Supper at Emmaus

Do we eat supper these days?
The couple on the Emmaus Road
knew it awaited them
they brought a friend
a well informed stranger
met on the way
a companion from Jerusalem
they thought
He reluctant and seeking not to impose
would have rejected their invitation
but pressed – agreed to share their fare:
bread, wine, fruit
Caravaggio caught the scene:
those astonished companions
recognising someone from somewhere
suddenly a familiar face: 'We know you!'
A 'met before' breaker of bread
a drinker of wine, a doppelganger
missing for three days
Walking down the Killucan Road
I saw the midnight sky
a mass of shooting stars –
We stopped. Sank down on a bank
and watched.
Things do happen
Miracles, mysteries, phenomena
As Caravaggio observed

David

A loud, hollow roar
thundered across the valley
defying – challenging
demanding of our armies
to put forth a man
just one man
to contest

There were plenty of men
my three brothers
who, though I brought them bread
scorned and scolded my presence

Striking fear and laughing
The uncircumcised
Goliath of Gath
appeared again
boasting

Can I not challenge
gather stones
throw
as at a bear or lion
embed them deep
within his brow?
Yes!

Narcissus in A and E

Across the narrow waiting room
You sat – apprehensive
Our bloods gone for testing
You waited: waited for the call, the results
Occasionally you stood up: flexed your muscles
Stretched, crouched, stretched again
Smoothed your black hair, re-set your pony-tail
In the mirroring door

Yes, we've noticed that noble frame
That fine physique, that so fair face
But then, by 2am it came, so suddenly
And came again and yet again and took your breath
That choking cough that brought you here
And shocked us all
Recovery came for an interlude
But still no doctor

A pale young man in the corner
Had a visit from friends
with burger and chips
A girl with a hole in her heart
went out for a smoke
Still the wait went on
all anxious, enduring, longing for sleep
Hippocrates diagnosed by smelling patients' sweat
We had to wait 'til dawn
When the bloods came back

Be Silent

Come in
Enter a most exclusive Order
Elijah, Ezekiel, Zechariah
They – and the Desert Fathers
will accompany you
These ones who knew silence invite you
to realms of depth and mystery

Stop your words
discover – in silence
God at work
Feel that incomprehensible presence
roused from a holy dwelling
responding to affliction
ready to speak

You'll need practise:
You'll want to leave
Decline – move away – repel
Stay
Sense an engagement
A meeting – and then:
An arrival

A Night On The Road

That day the climb was hard
the day hot, the back pack heavy
and the water sparse
Encouragement came as we thought of
the mountain village: O Cebriero
the pulpo, the chorizo, the wine and the bed
In the distance its bright lights signalled a welcome
slim dark figures moved against the mountain
joyful noises carried shared laughter
In the bar we ordered drinks
pilgrims, ready to tell their stories, sought our ear
No-one manned the desk where we waited
A scrubbed up pilgrim told the news
'The place is full; others have gone on...'
Disillusionment completed the day's
twenty-eight kilometres
Our guidebook suggested another 3k
would take us to Linares to a Casa Rural
'not pilgrim friendly'
Our stories and a bottle of wine
cheered the damp rooms
and microwaved food
At 6am our hostess, in her night attire,
watched us from her upstairs window as we left
without refreshment

Annie Laurie

Never heard of her – but the piece of paper
in the musical box, named her for the tune
He turned up with it one evening
and I pretended to like the tinny sound it made
I would have preferred some 'pop' music
Still, the thing itself had aesthetic quality
had the appearance of onyx – shiny
inlaid – with a coloured pattern on top
Inside its warm red lining held space
for jewellery and rings
It spent some years gathering dust
Came with me when I moved –
didn't use it – but occasionally
looked on with affection
After a while my new love noticed it
asked its history – saw it as a rival
– objected to its presence
feelings for the giver were long gone
my fondness was for the gift
Not wanting to make a stand I got rid of it
where to, I don't know –
In its silence it had said something
– nothing discernible
but, just like Annie Laurie
its presence had made an impact

Secrets

It was the trout soup
their Galician Grandam's legacy
now a house speciality
which brought people back:
attracted pilgrims to their Fonda
A recipe as old, they vowed
as Cervantes Bridge
straddling the Orbigo

The gathered family watched us eat
awaiting our response
They brought out the book, showed us
all satisfied customers
effulgent in their praise – of the trout soup
They persisted in their watching
throughout the second and third courses
communicating with smiles and a kind of love

But we, shamelessly
delighting in our own company
secretly longed to dismiss them

Sunday Afternoon in the City

"Got any change, please?"
Imaginary unspoken responses kick in
"Get a job!
You can walk!
Stop begging!"
At the shake of a head you went
but gave a backward look
reminiscent of someone I love
Repentant, I scanned the crowd

Just occasionally, unexpectedly
something touches the heart
Cupid's merciless arrow flies
the perfect opportune moment
ripe and full, is gone
The forelock of Kairos flees
and nothing but pain remains
Soon someone else will open a hand
while I, who loved for a moment
failed you

Bacchanalia

Is it your ignorance, Pentheus, that makes you unafraid
as you exult in kingly power – rejecting the god
heedless of consternation, alarm, amazement, dread
Would you indeed cast Semele's son into the net
in insolence bind him, take him
shear those sacred locks
that fall alluringly upon his cheeks
In folly and impiety, you act

Dionysus will instantly submit
indulge your strengthless humiliations
Then laugh at you, defy your threats
your weak intimidations
pronounce himself a god from Zeus's loins
prove his Lord's might and seize your willing women
Bacchants, playing wildly, they'll forget you
their husbands and their babes

Tasting the grape, their grief will disappear
their shyness fade, their inhibitions cease
High dignity and honour and all sweet innocence
meet with abandon, cherish the profligate
worship The Roaring One – dance to his tune
learn to see him – embrace his joy
kindle the flame, perform his rituals

You, Pentheus, King of Thebes,
your house shall shake, your pillars fall,
your sin of unbelief be manifest
Here is a god who makes high things low
And in disguise seeks out humility

Claude Lorraine:

—— The Marriage of Isaac and Rebekah ——

Claude - something inspired you
Was it a longing for simplicity?
A looking back to former times
An enticing landscape
A reading in Genesis
A glance towards the unpretentious
Or a low cost celebration?

Life went on
The herdsman watered his oxen
Little boats rested on the water
The mill wheel rolled
The piper played
And to the sound of tambourines
The lovers danced

But here was a world changing moment
A virgin, suitably pure, summoned from afar
Chosen and consecrated
Hereafter Matriarch of Nations
espoused to a tender Patriarch
Yes, consanguinity here
But that was how it was

The Short Day of the Chartists 1838–1857

(Preaching at Dodford Church, 2008)

Freedom from poverty was their aim
As they toiled
In their weakened state
In the name of liberty
For political reform
Spent what energy they had
seeking democracy
for the working classes
Dissenters
With their own Peoples' Charter:
'Land for the landless
votes for the disenfranchised'
Needing a living, a church
A better way of life

Looking at that outdoor pulpit now
What words were said in 1849?
Who stood and listened?
How were they dressed?
What was the weather like?
Were they warned?
Put in mind of Peterloo,
Of Corn Laws,
Of the Newport Rising
The Irish Famine
Tolpuddle?
Now the stuff of Key Stage 3 Social History

Moving On

Since you've been gone
you can't imagine what it's meant to me
Well, to my education mainly
I'm an ardent exponent of this life-long learning
but no longer willing to pay the price

With you around I retained it free of charge
It was an everyday occurrence
Over dinner, as we passed on the stairs
while you were on the phone
or looking out of a window
Even as you drove off
There's no replacing that, is there?

But hell, I started it all anyway, didn't I?
Made the introductions: Thucydides for one
History of the Peloponnesian War
it didn't take much
but there you are, that's the way it is

Now whose argument can sway my vote
Who'll exercise on me the latest 'speak'
Tell a truly subtle joke
pronounce the fate of some obscurist Pope
and know where the accent falls, on Córdoba?

Does she care who sacked Nimrud?
Why Orion pursues the Pleiades?
When Pliny the Younger wrote his Panegyricus
or in which direction the arrows travel
on a Byzantine map?

And is she able, at the end of the day
to secure for you, that last evasive cryptic clue?

Corpus Christi

It was the words 'Corpus Christi'
that delighted me
something mysterious
accompanied by a gift
a day off school!
I didn't need to know the meaning
straight after Mass the day was mine
Freedom!
No fearsome teachers
no inconstant friends
a long luxurious day
all mine

Circa 1450: Petrus Christus
oil on wood
had a different take:
there were thorns and gashes
trailing blood
the sword of justice
and the lilies of mercy
all working together
to bring me that day
of delight
'The man of sorrows'
five hundred years a focus of devotion
still going strong

Noise

Elijah stood –
Waited for something – on Mount Horeb
A ferocious wind enveloped the mountains
Cracked the fissures, ran along the grain
Encouraged an earthquake
Lent bellows to a spark
Added terror to abject fear

Elijah stood –
No psychological projection here
No shifting of blame
No questioning
No looking for why

Elijah stood – before the Lord
In the silence
Listened
Heard the still small voice
The gentle whisper of peace
That waited –
Waited patiently to speak

Pygmalion and Galatea

Choice was the challenge from the start
the un-carved blocks:
one by one rejected
Too rough, too big, too small, a hairline fracture
'til the right one came along

The brightness of the day inspired a first chip
and got a response
proving so easy
Shoulders began to form:
strong, gentle, expressive
inclining forward
merging with a perfect torso
and arms:
so smooth, graceful, expressive

Spring turned to the heat of summer
as finer definitions surfaced:
delicate hands, sensitive fingers
broke through pale ivory
silently responding
as to a lover

Sweat trickled down a grimed face:
the heart began to palpitate
Days swept by encouraging labour
creative hours enthralled
delight ran rampant

The neck and breasts unfolded perfectly
a deep breath preceding those nipples
a belly so fine and legs so comely
then that back, those tender curves
and last of all that face divine

New days dawned
and languishment and yearning
Some fierce desire to touch:
while sternest decency demands refrain

Venus still honoured
still shows a heart
that loves the pure
And with her beauteous Spirit fires
With life – and satisfies desire

Search The Fields

Roll up! Roll up! It's all here
For every question an answer
A whole database
At least 1,200 solutions and more
What's your subject?
Search the field use the key words
they'll take you there
get a PhD lying in bed

Why then do we live in this dichotomy
between hope and despair?
What's wrong? What do we yet need
to help us want to go on living
to cope to be happy?
How are we to understand the enigma
is there an answer to that?
Surely there are at least 1,200 to consider
apart from Edvard Munch's cosmic Scream

Seminar

Clustered in a small room
The seeming Holy Innocents
looking tired
In torn jeans and crazy tee shirts
awaiting the unwary text
Their Apollo holds the reins:
keeping them at bay
He lets them loose – they fall
male and female alike
– voracious
rending, clawing, lacerating
Drawn back again – redressed
they hold the scent
Only to fall once more
And leave fragmented flesh
strewn around
with broken teeth
and bloodied chops

The Year:

—— Another Morning in the Head of ... ——

5.20am. On the right station
The lull of the shipping forecast sounds
News, papers, sport
In touch with the world
Eagerly awaiting... 5.43
In hope of spiritual food... a re-awakening
Someone else to do the work
To uplift, to teach, to satisfy
A prayer for the day

5.45... 'Farming Today' rutting deer at Woburn
We should eat more venison
7am, still dark... wait awhile
The 'stern daughter' kicks in
Morning Office?
or maybe 9.45... Daily Service?
Someone else to do the work
Bringing the plight of the destitute
To the Mercy Seat
I'll join in

10am... The Martin Luther sermon calls
That's good... those 95 theses
On the door at Wittenberg
Shouting 'liberty'!
I can do that
Is good enough really good enough?

To R.S. Thomas

I find you bleak
Speaking a reality I don't want to hear
Of a God found in flintiness
Austere, ascetic, Spartan
The God of the hair shirt
Exacting penance
Cold, indifferent, apathetic

And yet although his eyes are shut
You plead his cause
Make us aware
Of the hill farmer's calloused hands
The delicate movement
Of a child in the womb
A receding star
The significance of
A dying lamb

Even you, steely enough
While dashing your prayers
Against the cliff's face
Open your ear
To the cry of the robin
Pity the moth
Speak of love and truth
Attempt a repairing of the soul
Break through the severity
And for today release a healing

Underground

It's 3.45am – there's a sound
It's water splashing
The radio's still on
Beneath the Derbyshire Dales
an enthusiastic tunneller
describes his lifelong passion

An awed interviewer asks questions –
cautiously journeys – mentions wellies
I drift in and out of the tunnel
feeling my way – afraid
hating the darkness
enduring a desperation

Eventually – I hear a gem
'I've noticed',
the fellow tunneller says:
'That no matter how long
or dark the tunnel is –
there's always a shaft of light
at the end'

Grub Street

It was ever the same
The three P's: Princes, Power and Prices
The stuff of the journalist
Forcing its way to the front
as Names, Money, Power

Grub Street. 19th century London.
The place to be
Among the Bohemians learning a trade
Here with writers and poets
In squalor and impoverishment
Digging superficially

Searching all the time
In Joe Lyons' café society
With so many literary hacks
Waiting for a story
Ready to shame wrongdoing, injustice
London's multitudinous crimes
Ever the same

Mardi Gras At Queens

How shockingly unexpected
finding You
there
in the dance
Spirit of awareness
and communion
breaking in
on formality
and reserve
inviting abandon

Here
no primitive suspicion
shameful distrust
or apprehension
but a new You
unsought
immersed
gloriously alive
for me
in the dance

Othello

No foreboding – the return was joyous
into that Cyprian port
anticipation calming every nerve
after a perilous journey through those raging seas
whose desperate tempests
sought to menace and prevent

No word from a Cassandra
no siren, foghorn, beacon light
to warn of condemnation
but longing and ambition
for honeyed nights
and love's embrace

But tragic flaws
in all men's lives
come forward one by one
and drag the chaffed
and wrangled heart
unpitied to despair

Letters

The years of application gave him a fine hand
Copperplate they called it
When he went to the office at twelve years of age
Too smart, they said, for the pit, too smart
So he took the blue collar and entered their ledgers
But no, men went underground - and came up black
So he shared their life of hardship, below and above
Strikes and disasters - soup kitchens and poverty
And he - like the ancient Scribe
Committed to paper their grievances
The rejected plea - for an extra shilling
Discussed in the Blue Pig
Disappointingly unclaimed for war:
signs of deafness; chest not good
"Go home to your Mother"!
And the heartache of deceit and a broken marriage
But a family to write to in that fine hand
Telling of a still strong faith and a life well lived
And the ones who, in the darkness, lie there still

For Sale

The time is ripe to downsize!
A viewer of the video is impressed –
observing golfers from the Juliette balcony
But knocking an internal wall he comments:
'This isn't brick'! And quickly left
Others oo-d and ahh-d – admiring the garden
then made ridiculously low offers
Two Medical Consultants, sparing an hour
came one Sunday
spent half the visit upstairs – discussing
Their complaint was the traffic
Another claimed the garage dominated the house
All the time we were unworried
Take it or leave it – it's OK with us
But underneath there is an attachment
the ups of Christmases, summer parties
conversations
route planning – packing for long treks
Flourishing foliage and cherished apple trees –
Returning wrens and robins
notoriously ill-behaved squirrels –
a bench with history, a gazebo that began with hope
home to a honeysuckle that won't co-operate
And the downs heartbreak, tears, the occasional row
But as for the walls – so sorry they're not brick
But what there is – is soaked with prayer
May I suggest that like Moses
you take off your shoes?

Untitled

It hadn't been a warm day
Quite raw in fact
They kept the stove on in school
On the way home we had an ice lolly
Green they were, elongated
Worth walking a bus stop for
The jokes we told each other
Weren't very good
Some funny, some dirty
Some without a punch line
From our gate I could see a wardrobe
It was outside the closed front door
There was a woman there
Sitting on a chair with her blouse open
Feeding a baby
There were some men there
Looking strong but helpless
And our chest of drawers
And my Mum
I've always loved words
I learned a new one that day
Eviction

What is it but Nightfall?

We set out from Succoth
Carrying Joseph's bones
A large company in fear and awe
The might of Egypt conquered
Defeated, disappointed, drowned

From children questions came
Others seized with consternation
Accompanied by doubt, interrogated:
Where are we going... what will happen
Can we not go back, darkness is falling

Is there a god of night who waits to hear
One who courts invocation, living sacrifice
To whom we could present our 'plaint
Already faith begins to melt
And hearts sink down in hopelessness

A few remained unmoved
Steadfast, silent, tenacious
Was it their response
That stirred the All-powerful Clemency
To send protection:
A pillar of cloud by day
A pillar of fire by night

Oedipus

O dire awakening
doomed arousal
headache and inertia scattering

that your fine stones
Colonus
might now cry out:

shame! agony! despair!

turn back! turn back!
deny exsistence
O spare my loves

yet that sweet one
in faithfulness sublime
remake inviolate

come Desolation
see me!
wretched! duped! and blind!

and worse
an inward blindness
which failed to recognise

and known
unknown
engendered infamy

Furniture

The chest of drawers was, of late, a bachelor's
Top left, although hardly level with the right
contained and smelt of:
Brylcreem, polish and lighter fuel

It was wrought in the finest mahogany
with large matching knobs
that fell off at times
and dull redundant keyholes

As a family it was one of our few possessions
and on Saturdays we made it shine
If anyone came to stay they were allotted a drawer
and coloured paper was placed at the bottom

Occasionally a neighbour would borrow a drawer
and we would see a baby sleeping soundly in its embrace
It has to be said it was one of the constants of our lives
in an otherwise unstable existence
Unnoticed, as we began to prosper, it left us

Curious

In monochrome
and staring at me from the small screen
My school friends from long ago
With text added their memories raced
'I was there in '56, I was there in '65...
Do you remember...?
Mr Hayhurst: 'Composition' on a Tuesday
all of us in love with him
Miss Kelly, and rote learning of
'The Quality of Mercy...'
while listening to Dvorzak
Mr Seeney, young, teaching French
La fenêtre, le mur, la porte...'
It was a lovely school - was it?
A Head 'strict but fair' they said - yes
We had a good education - yes, indeed
Here was one ex-pupil from America
with a list of accolades
another from the Azores
Our motto was remembered:
'Look up and Aim High'
Schools Reunite can disturb
I joined in and like the foolish teenager I was
talked too much

The Bannister

At one time
the house was a status symbol
right side of town
space for a family
impressive entrance: oak bannister
fine garden, rhubarb and an apple tree
all hard earned

The plaque tells the rest
Otto's family lived here: 1901
His wife's sister joined them
their children grew up
some went, some stayed
Jacob was born here in 1931
and Etty in '35

The years become ominous
their home a ghetto
full of frightened families
up and down those stairs
'til the day of silence

For the present inhabitants
there has been restoration:
a coat of paint
some new doors
but that garden – surely it is still the same
and that bannister
unrestored, original
down which those families ran
holding on

Basil

Good Friday In Bromsgrove

I'd never thought of Jesus
as old before:

vigorous
sociable
friend
revolutionary
carpenter
son
brother
healer
priest
prophet
king
lord
human
divine
leader
servant
teacher
Jew
Saviour:

but not old
not 'til today
when I saw Basil's face

it was his turn to carry the cross
he looked tired
needed help

took a rest as a hymn was sung
eyes closed
leaning forward
sorrowful

Christ – free in time
unrestricted
broke through
showed Himself
once again
left His mark
there today:
on that face

Stanley Spenser: Tidying

How fascinating!
A resurrection morning
In 'everyday' style
People waking up
overwhelmed with joy!

Spotting friends and neighbours
health and strength renewed
Running, laughing, touching
Quite unafraid

Others – enemies of old
deep in conversation
Loving, smiling, sharing
this new found peace

Gaping graves redundant
throwing up their dead
Into life eternal
and heavenly embrace

Here the extraordinary
rejoices in the ordinary
And best of all:
sisters comb each others hair
just the way it always was

Remembering

'He could do with a hat on a cold day like this...'
so I thought as I watched him there
underneath a tree

he was early in position just left of the cenotaph
at the back of the dais
somewhat out of the way

when we all fell silent he kept his head bowed

I was distracted myself
the woman behind complaining,
the dog in front alerted,
by the blast of gunfire

as we began to sing:
'O God our help in ages past...'
he turned around on his stick
took his hat out of his pocket
and picked his way slowly
through the gravestones

Moral Clarity

There is no new vocab.
always a disappointment
we're running with:
illegal, immoral, unjust
and grave responsibility
although precision weaponry
falls smoothly

Callously speaking
the hopeful thing
is that P.M. commitment:
'the safeguarding of
archaeological treasures:
we want them intact
that is important to us'

For now though
there's a humanitarian crisis
with aerial bombardment
disaster, devastation and death
but the strangest thing of all
is that talk
of a true and lasting peace

... and a highway shall be there

Isaiah Ch. 35 v. 8

Prepare yourself for a Utopia
or a Nirvana
A state of blissful tranquillity
when the prophet's words come true

On this highway there will be
no mindless rioters
drunken Fathers or Mothers
the violent or deceivers

You can walk this road without alarm
No ravenous beast shall fill you with dread
threaten your life or weaken your spirit
in this place of confidence

There will be none without eyes, ears or tongue
None limping; no lack of water or food
in this blossoming desert
but soundness and strength shall be for all
On this highway

A Knowledge of ...

The beach holiday was somewhat lacking:
surrounded as it was by a mass of ageing flesh
baking away from day to day
sleeping, snorting, rubbing down

The selected reading for the duration again fell short
Too few books
Too much time
No Kindle
As the psalmist cried, 'from where is my help to come?!'

Salvation arrived in the form of a newsfeed:
A regular alert signed up to long ago
Neglected, and often – if truth be known –
Spurned

But here it was: noticed, appreciated, ready to inspire!
This stuff must surely be for the weird among us
None other than – wait for it...
'Aristotle's Theory of Epistemology!'
heaven on a hotel computer

Take a lesson:
Next time
apart from the 50 block
realise the need to be 'out of your depth'

A Deadly Sin

Sloth – is that a lack of discipline in the mind
A failure to adopt the positive attitude
The absence of a list of 'must do's'
A sighing and a turning over in the bed
A sense of fatigue
A battle lost

Or is it just a caving in – a primitive reaction
of full surrender to the enormity of life's assaults
An alluring portico to oblivion
A lack of determination to fight anymore
An indulgence and an engagement
with that modern sin of pessimism

Accusations – from self or elsewhere
Serve only to increase languidity
And conquer in their persistence
It becomes harder and harder
To hold a shield and lift a spear:
to raise a helmeted head

Tomorrow –
where active combat will surely commence
becomes a friend
A far off time devoid of ennui
Possessed of something, some meaning
Where lassitude has no realm
And triumph armed with vigour waits

Plato's Cave

Imprisoned from birth
Chained and untutored
Closed minds watch
Straight ahead
Deceptive images
In Plato's cave

Shadows falling on a wall
False images of Reality
Cast by mendacious teachers
Demanding "Look to the front!"
Turn those heads – see the Real
Become a philosopher!

Mrs Beeton

Come and view
One of Solomon's virtuous women
Working with willing hands
Teaching the generations
The art of jugging a hare
Of buying a house
Of raising a sponge

And more – childcare, animal husbandry
Fashion and religion
Class, gender roles
Thrift and cleanliness
Not forgetting her soup
"For benevolent purposes"
To the poor of Pinner

Like the good wife
Strength and dignity clothed her
While childbearing and miscarriages
Bore witness to modern suspicions
Of a not so virtuous husband
At twenty eight – she closed those virtuous eyes

Kinnegad c1929

Was it a Sunday afternoon
That time between
Mass and dinner
when women are in the house
and the young have nothing to do?

You still in your good clothes
collar off, relaxed, with friends
caught in the youthful moment
at social ease
together

all the rest lay ahead
she – to meet the English soldier
who thought he was the lucky one
well, they all wanted her,
but not you

You. Upright. Decent.
Waiting for something, waiting
And it came, a proper wife
Just the job
As you used to say

Babushka

Look, this is the basic story
I'm called, old woman, grandmother
And, since 1963, Babushka Lady

The Steppes are always cold
Rheumatism arrives early
Starting in the legs
But it was a once in a lifetime...

Just the one chance
And that not taken
Too cold
Too busy
Too painful

And those Wise Men
With time to look at the stars
Yes, I gave hospitality
Had an offer to go with them
But they were energetic, young
Stronger than their beasts
Would they wait for me?

I, though free in time
Will never reach that destination
Nor claim a place in the tableau
There was just the one chance
And that not taken
Too tired
Too cold
Too busy

Hidden God

Why is it all so extreme
Is there something we don't understand?
I search for meaning
people suffer
we do our best
we still fail
Why?
There must be some reason
It's all a great puzzlement

Going somewhere
is that what it's about?
The kind of thing Clov speaks of:
'something taking its course'
all of us involved
in the great Tribulation
the bringing forth of something:
like a birth

O the discipline
the endurance
the participation
the patience
the pain

We'll have to wait that's all

Expecting something
To be happy, peaceful
to have the good
the right to be indignant
Why all the secrecy
is that your way
are you protecting us
are we not yet the Nietzsche man
capable of eye contact
sharing the truth?

Ash Wednesday

It always looks shameful
That mark
On other people
As though they are to blame
For something
Even for accepting it
And leaving it there

Come today then
Experience this humiliation
Just like ancient Israelite
And Babylonian kings
Degraded
Receiving their annual blows
Atoning for the people

It's about being afflicted then
And in that state to make intercession
Does some sense dawn
Can we make comparisons
Will today make a difference
That mark being borne
And when You see
Will You forgive?

Josie

Credo in unum Deum...
Sixteen years a chorister
Standing behind a pillar
That's ok, no complaint
Thursday nights: practise the skill
Friday afternoons: arrange the flowers
Patrem omnipotentem factorem caeli et terrae
Here to serve:
Be a wife, be a mother
Go to confession
Pray for others
Light a candle
Credo in unum Dominum Jesum Christum
Take the path through the year: observe the fasts
the feasts, the festivals
Sanctus, Sanctus, Sanctus
Nowadays it's hard to remember
To remember
In conversation repeating the same news
Forgetting birthdays
Irritating loved ones
Rejecting visitors
Happy enough cloistered
Tending the garden
Hermitical
De Profundis clamavi ad te Domine
Out of the depths I cry to You...

The Cousins: Lily and Nellie

They shared our home for a while
and our bedroom
Their method for getting
us to sleep was simple:
'Will Power' – don't be the first to speak

Creative poetry was their thing
in the oral tradition
All unaware they had a natural cadence
and respect for semantics
We were entertained in iambic pentameter

On Sundays they took us to the 12 o'clock Mass
They would never get up for the 9.30
Afterwards they took us to a little café
for eggs and bacon, along with Nellie's boyfriend
George – who was a bus-driver

Having helped us discover the beauty of silence
and the delights of the iambus
they left us
Lily went to Australia
and Nellie worked on the buses

Jephtah

They spoke:
My half-brothers
The despisers
Having banished me from home
I the son of our father Gilead
and a prostitute
who left me at his door
The land of Tob embraced me
I made a home in Mizpah

They spoke again:
Return, lead us, take command
defeat the Ammonites
who breathe their threats
I despised such brothers – and yet

I spoke
Made a vow:
If victory favours me
On my return
I will sacrifice
as a burnt offering
whatever comes out of my door

I wept:
tore my clothes
Alas Alas! my only child
with timbrel and dance welcomed me
O my daughter, my daughter!
O my heart, my heart!

It Is the Arts!

Abstract Expressionism challenges us
to abandon physicality
To enter the nothingness
A potent welcoming nothingness
That questions the elaborate minutiae
Of being

Here – find a new something
relieve the spiritual emptiness
Lose yourself – meet yourself
You, the painting, and maybe
Another
A Trinity of Being

Abandon the nothingness
Come back
To a different something
Revived, unbridled
Optimistic:
A loss and a gain

Ideas

The Preacher told us long ago:
'There's nothing new under the sun'
Teaching with cynicism:
he mocked this meagre strand of life
called it meaningless, futile, fruitless
gave us a call to indulgence
to living insecurely for the day
embracing the absence of order or purpose

Are all our ideas just a re-mix?
getting out, as someone said
a new can of paint?
Where do ideas come from?
generated, surely, by our wild, unconquered
imagination
willing to ignore the pleas of reason
taking the risk – approving recklessness
meeting success with something novel
Yet – failing to harmonize with the Cosmic Order

Jan Vermeer: The Kitchen Maid

See how the light falls
On that Madonna, Priest-Servant
With rolled up sleeves
And hoisted skirt
The gentleness
The strong supporting hand
Engulfed in the silence
Work made holy
By the Zen of concentration
And blends of subtle colour
Bringing richness out

O Silentium Mysterium
Will that bread sing
That cheese weep
That wine bring glory?

Marriage

What is it that takes control
makes eyes meet
to cunningly indulge a lingering gaze
suggesting a new, a threatening blaze
luring the incautious heart
to miss a beat?
Leading on –
do you take this woman, to have, to hold?
excitedly engaging in the dream –
the rashness of youth
major commitments, pledges, duties –
fickle words of truth
delighting for a moment
in the cherished band of gold
Soon cynicism grows –
disillusions worm away, meet a harsh reality
Still, still, a revitalising touch remains
assuring of comfort, confirming mutuality
An inviting hand reaches out in love
meets an accepting hand
a constant gaze
the promised blessing from above

The Sacred Oak of Mamre

In the shade of the terebinth
With the sun at its highest
I was outside my tent
Resting
In the distance three figures loomed
Footsore, they seemed, and weary
Compassion swelled in me
I ran to them

Let me wash your feet – refresh you
Lay a table before you
Stay a while – take some food
Tell your news

These messengers – were they angels?
History will say so
To me, three men in need
Now, veiled conveyers
Sons are hard to come by
But Sarah will have one
So they said
Next year

Passed them in the Halls

In those places of learning that have meant so much
Especially the libraries
A community, elite, and generally, reflective
I pass through these places, loving the quiet
Respecting the scholarship
aware of my shortcomings
The friends I've made, the way we've helped
And inspired each other
Been there in the hard times
delighted in the good times
Prayed for each other, wished each other well
How different the early days
when competition was the thing
Marks were all the talk: what did you get?
'O, an alpha'
And you...? Not quite
I could walk those halls forever,
seeking wisdom searching for answers
Wanting to please...someone
There's always 'someone' who requires something
The one who can make the judgement
Cheer or depress you for three weeks
Help you get nearer
To those ones who know how to critique
argue the case
Show originality, take the right stance
Be acceptable

Perseus

What danger there is
In being pre-occupied with beauty

Cassiopeia
Boastful Queen of the Ethiopians
Claimed to exceed the Nerieds
All fifty daughters of the deep
And one of them Achilles mother!

They complained
And Poseidon made
Andromeda to suffer
Chained to a rock
The sacrificial price of pride
Reluctant to confess
that it was all her mother's fault!

No wonder, is it then, that Perseus
Having suffered drenched wings
and snapping jaws
to save her
Gave Andromeda new bonds
And Cassiopeia a place in the sky
Forever in a state
of compromise!

Scholastica to Benedict

A dedicated maiden, I dare not lift my eyes
But you, brother, twin, monk, ever sharpen my call
Embodying my love for the divine
Your visits assuage my longing,
My ache, my throbbing, my hungry soul

Here, in my convent,
Near the fire we talk, lost in a reverie
Time evaporating,
You must go. You always must go
But stay, this one night
Listen to my plea
Indulge a beloved sister

Could not you
So single minded, so dedicated to love and wisdom
forget your monastery for just one night
to help me soar to realms celestial
To re-ignite the flame that weakly flickers
Listen. Stay. But no. You won't.

The piteous window starts to cloud
A storm arises, snow falls
My silent prayer was heard
by the all-seeing, all hearing, Almighty
But not by you Brother
Now the choice is not yours
You must stay. Hallelujah!

Westhill

Like its residents Archibald house
was welcoming
On the ground floor lodged the college library
whose guardians, in their very being
spoke a piercing silence
The upper floors held students
whose doors were always open
offering coffee, enjoying converse
so polite, so political, so opinionated
The views from the windows spanned the seasons
with blues and greens and yellows
pinks, reds, bronzes
and gnarled oaks withstanding another winter
Below, a lawned terrace spread
and there, in summer, we would lie and read
Nearby was the chapel
Where we met in times of stress
We were the insiders: the ones who read theology
the 'rare birds' as they said
People who imagined a caring God, a Guide
to whom we told our truths, divulged our weaknesses
as fearful teachers in embryo
preparing to transform the world

Catalogue

I loved that dress
White with blue and
green spots

"Blue and green should
never be seen"
Nevertheless

And the material
so soft
And the shape
so smooth
And me
disguised

It was the way the world worked
One shilling a week

In Post-war Britain
we learned to wait
Disappointment was rare
We had few expectations

Occasionally
an unspoken dream
was realised

Me in the dress
So soft
So smooth
So prophetic

Romeo

From my balcony I see him
Waiting in the wings
No velvet doublet – inviting touch – today
But shirt and jeans
For yet another virgin Romeo

From my balcony I see him
What would he say if he guessed my thoughts?
"I have a partner, I'm married
Don't confuse me
Be detached, objective
The play's the thing"

From my balcony I see him
Mouthing his lines so charmingly
Careless of real unwritten passion
Which watches, waits and schemes
Determining a way

From my balcony I see him
Ready to take the stage
With one who knows these lines
And can so easily beguile
The hungry watchers
In their stalls

From my balcony I see him
With such commanding presence:
All innocent and guileless
All's fair... they say
So be assured, my Romeo, a Capulet shall triumph
O'er a Montague
And you shall fall – headlong
To a plump and aging Juliet

Paris

Lunching al-fresco
in view of the Eiffel Tower
Then to visit Sacre-Coeur
A cruise along the Seine
See the Tuileries
The Latin Quarter
Notre Dame
The Louvre
What a day!

Out for the evening
Dressed up
The black outfit and earrings
The fine restaurant
Running to get the train
But....

Opposite us a young man
Oriental in appearance
With dark embryo moustache
And eyes cast down
The face of humility

See blue canvas shoes
With holes at the toes
Beneath his arm
unsold sketches
His whole being
Personifying poverty

Porte d'Orleans
Time to get off!
Along the platform
He follows
Quick words exchange
"Give him some money
He needs some food!"

The reverse turn
and guilt-ridden offering
startled him
Fear crossed his face
An attempt at French
With gestures
"Vous obtenez de la nourriture"
'You get some food'

And then a glorious smile
of gratitude
The blessing of the poor
Love's reward

Tarmac

A careless slip on ice
Then slow motion
As the head took a backward
route
Down towards a violent bounce
And another one

Then a lying still
A desire to stay forever
Unmoving, absorbed in earth
Contemplating trees
Blue skies beyond

Unknown giant figures and a dog
look down
Emanating a tenderness
Entering my world
Longing to help
a stranger

The Spirit Level

The new skirting board was planned
It would take a whole evening
more possibly
Mostly we watched
But were not barred from engaging
We passed the tools required
And agreed that the work was good
Problems arose with lack of attention
If a screw driver was required
It had to be the right size
But the real centre of learning that evening
Was the use of the Spirit Level
Testing the accuracy of wood on wall
The task was delegated, the privilege
granted:
"Check if it's straight"
"Yes, it is"
 Another check revealed the truth:
"Do you call that straight?"
"Well no... not really"
"Bring the tapping hammer"
 A couple of taps and a summons to
 re-check
"Yes, it's straight"
"Remember that then"

Pericles Style

Any gifts, perfumes?
They approach
with voices that deny
the resistant mindset
How much is it anyway
thirty pounds?
In these circumstances
why do I always think of
Third World starving children
charities ignored and
Long overdue donations
to the Leprosy Mission?
Are you short of perfume, love.
Do you need any?
Need any?
Who the hell needs perfume, I don't!
What about all those years
of deprivation?
Why, O why, do we go on perpetuating
our wartime mentality?
It'll just have to go down
Pericles style:
'essential expenditure'
I can afford it
I can afford a thousand damn bottles!
Yes, Chanel No.5, please
Is that large or small Madam?

Visit to the British Museum

Xenophon!

How could you just walk past
the walls of Nineveh
Pride of Assyria

benevolent Spirits opposing evil
guarding portals
monstrously

stamped – bearing forever
the strain .
of the age

telling tales – frightful still
of cities stormed
armies routed

Assurbanipal's
absolute monarchy
exalted

forgetting Lilith who in her hand
carries that short rope
of mortality

Virtuality

Omar Khayyam thought it through
(circa twelfth century C.E.)
Mortality is the problem
he talks about 'knots of human fate'
It's not easy to cope with

Sisters, brothers in community
for instance,
order their day strictly
The discipline of prayer, silence, work
all join together to make meaning

It's having someone in charge
temporal and ultimate authority
calling the tune, giving safety
Your future in capable hands
liberty hidden away in obedience

The meaning always, always, in the waiting
just like in R. S. Thomas or Becket
Lives that dare to hope
faithfully expecting an outcome
a breaking through to something new

Reunion

Thirty years it's been
you there, living, waiting
still, what was is yet
though passed and gone
What a mystery!

Back you came. Haunting
reminding attracting inspiring
weakening absorbing
creating again
those times

Old passions lie buried
and unexpected reappear
that I awe filled
can stare – and suffer
once more

Herbert – the Philippino

The theme was poverty
we see clear evidence every day
Herbert's was somehow different
he owned it

A young child working on the land
early mornings and late evenings
weekends spent...
cleaning the owner's house

These are resented memories
which questioned, even then,
injustice:
"Why do we do the work
and he takes the food?"

An hour's walk to school
and back again
the same lunch every day
dried rice and salt fish
eaten, for shame's sake,
apart

It was indeed a home
with his grandparents
in that bamboo hut
but could hardly be called
a house

One-day unfairness was
transformed:
the education worked
and the dried rice and salt fish too
both feeding defiant thoughts

Now a vindicator
a someone
who, knowing and feeling
the sting of injustice
takes their part
and fights
so eloquently - for others

Herbert –
Mysterious are the routes
to priesthood
bring your certificate
and when you get home
we'll hang it on the wall.

Agamemnon

Yes Horace
I agree

I agree there were
there were heroes
before Agamemnon

yet he, he
Majesty, loath
loath to tread purple

Mycenae! Mycenae!
how you lie

he knew! he knew!
the greater you are
the more the more
lowliness

everything everything
comes to nothing